Colorful
Northern
California

Colorful
Northern
California

PHOTOGRAPHY BY: ED COOPER, STEVE CROUCH, BOB CLEMENZ, TOM MYERS, ROY MURPHY, AND TOM TRACY

Text by William Curran

Published by Beautiful West Publishing Company
202 N.W. 21st, Portland, Oregon 97209
Robert D. Shangle, Publisher

First Printing

ISBN 0-915796-32-5
ISBN 0-915796-31-7 (Paperback edition)

CONTENTS

PHOTO CREDITS 6

INTRODUCTION 7

THE MOUNTAINS 10

NORTH CALIFORNIA MAP 15

THE COAST 18

THE LAKES 58

THE VALLEY 66

SAN FRANCISCO AND THE BAY AREA 70

CREDITS

Lithography by Sweeney, Krist & Dimm, Portland, Oregon
Bindery by Lincoln and Allen Company, Portland, Oregon
Type by AAA Composition, Portland, Oregon

PHOTO CREDITS

Ed Cooper: *page 13; page 24, bottom; page 25; page 26; page 27, top; page 27, bottom; page 28, bottom; page 32-33; page 38; page 39, top; page 40; page 41, top; page 44, top; page 45; page 46, top; page 48-49; page 50; page 51, top; page 52; page 53; page 54, top; page 54, bottom; page 55; page 60; page 61, top; page 61, bottom; page 64; page 65; page 68, top; page 69, top; page 69, bottom left; page 69, bottom right; page 72; cover; back cover.*

Steve Crouch: *page 20, top; page 20, bottom; page 21; page 24, top; page 30, top; page 30, bottom; page 31; page 34; page 35, top; page 35, bottom; page 36, top left; page 36, top right; page 36, bottom right; page 41, bottom; page 56, top; page 56, bottom; page 68, bottom.*

Bob Clemenz: *page 9; page 28, top; page 36, bottom left; page 42-43; page 44, bottom; page 46, bottom; page 47; page 51, bottom; page 69, top left.*

Roy Murphy: *page 12; page 29; page 39, bottom; page 57.*

Tom Tracy: *page 37.*

Tom Myers: *page 16-17.*

INTRODUCTION

CALIFORNIA! An ancient and tired joke says that it is not a state but a state of mind. The name, "California," has probably stirred more emotion in the breasts of Americans than has any other except "America" itself. For almost a century and a half those emotions have been largely positive, pleasurable excitement at the thought of a land wholly new, beautiful, and rich. Such feelings gave birth to epithets like El Dorado and the Golden State. In recent decades some of the feeling about California has turned to denigration and hostility. Concerning California, it seems, neutrality is impossible.

Curiously, California has never generated the same vision in all men. To the pretty, unemployed Chicago typist in the 1920s, the Oklahoma farmer in the 1940s, and the restless Brooklyn war veteran in the late 1940s, it almost certainly meant the Los Angeles basin, with its plentiful sunshine, its beaches, its citrus groves, its 20th-century industries like motion pictures, aircraft construction, electronics. To the Ohio farm boy of the 19th century, however, California could only have meant the mother lode country of the Sierra foothills or a slower kind of riches drawn from the warm soil of the central valley.

People within the state have long recognized two Californias. Geologically, it may be argued that Northern California extends as far south as Point Conception and the entrance to the warm Santa Barbara Channel. On the other hand, social attitudes associated with Southern California are readily observed as far north as Carmel and Fresno. Although this book is intended as a record of the beauties of Northern California, it does not claim to define exact boundaries between the two.

People in the north charge that Southern Californians are insensitive to the beauties of nature, that they are wanton despoilers of the environment. Such a sweeping indictment is unfair and almost certainly untrue. What is true is that in Northern California, nature lovers and conservationists have been visible, vocal, and well organized for more than a century. There should be nothing surprising in this, since few people in history have had so much worth preserving. From the once heavily-timbered coast to the deep blue bowl of Lake Tahoe, from Shasta's peak to Monterey Peninsula, the California first seen by Americans must have been a land of heart-stopping beauty. The Americans have taken their toll of this beauty, it is true, but thanks to the foresight and selflessness of a few, much beauty remains intact, as the photos in this book attest.

Intoxicated by life in a demi-paradise, some Northern Californians early developed an Arcadian mentality and a consequent fear that coarse and insensitive newcomers could bring a swift end to the good life. The roots of this feeling can be seen in the reported reluctance of Captain John Sutter to disclose that gold had been discovered at his mill and the private revelation in his diary that "At once . . . the curse of the thing burst upon my mind." Sutter did eventually lose all his land to gold-crazed intruders and died penniless. His tragic history has not been lost on later generations of Northern Californians. And so the dream of Arcadia persists, fueled by the undeniable fact that Northern California has the natural wealth to go it alone.

As recently as 1975, Ernest Callenbach of Berkeley published an utopian novel, *Ecotopia,* about a secessionist republic of that name, embracing Northern California, Oregon and Washington. The major, and virtually the sole, national policy of Ecotopia is to maintain a society living in harmony with nature and dedicated to the perpetuation of natural beauty. Significantly, when Callenbach's Ecotopians revolt from the U.S., they covet no territory south of Monterey.

Visions of Ecotopias notwithstanding, the two Californias are, in the words of the marriage ceremony, joined together "for better or for worse." They have no choice but to face the future together and like George and Martha in the play, they may come to agree that they wouldn't have it any other way.

In this book, the contributions of six photographers sum up the prodigious and infinitely varied beauty of the region. Brilliant as they are, photos can offer but a suggestion of actuality. But there should be in this record a note of reassurance for us all, Californians and visitors alike. Whatever course the state's political and economic history may take, much of the beauty of the place is likely to survive. It may prove the most enduring capital.

(Opposite:) Viewed from the snow covered banks of Merced River, majestic Half-Dome in Yosemite National Park stands out as a familiar landmark.

THE MOUNTAINS

NORTHERN CALIFORNIA is a land of mountains. In reasonably clear weather, there is probably no spot in the region out of visible range of a peak, a ridge, a rounded headland. In poetic terms, Northern California is a child of its mountains. Without them, it might be another Libya, with 100 thousand square miles of desert sands continuing to the edge of the sea.

On the coast north of Eureka, rainfall is heavy. The central valley, on the other hand, doesn't get nearly enough. It remains for the tall peaks of the Cascades and the High Sierras to wring additional moisture from the winds in the form of snow. Later, this water finds its way back to the valley through the mountain streams and the river system. Since they also shield California from the frigid winter winds of the continental interior, the high mountains prove a double blessing.

Mountain ranges in Northern California generally run north-south, the prevailing pattern in the Western Hemisphere. At the northern end of the state, small transverse ranges like the Salmon Mountains link the larger chains.

The Coast Range, or more accurately ranges, extend as far north as the Olympic Peninsula of Washington and could be described in Northern California as the "habitable mountains." Most of the population — and this includes that of San Francisco — already lives within the limits of the range. With elevations averaging just a couple of thousand feet, the coastal mountains are suitable for farming, cattle grazing, winemaking, dairying, and — growing in importance — outdoor recreation.

South of San Francisco, agriculture along the coast is in slow retreat. Fields that once produced artichokes, broccoli, or Brussels sprouts are giving way to golf courses and housing developments. North and south of the Bay Area, the premium wine country is still holding its own. It remains to be seen whether Californians will ever be ready to sacrifice good wine for row houses.

Estimates are that by the year 2000, the state's population may be 40 million or more. Most of these millions are likely to be within the coastal mountains. The region may begin to resemble Italy. That's not an unpleasant prospect.

In contrast to the populated Coast Range, the Warner Mountains in the northeast corner of the state are in part a wilderness area. For backpackers, the Warners may well offer the maximum solitude possible within the state borders.

The photogenic peaks of the Cascade Range stretch as far north as the Canadian Border. They don't occupy much of Northern California but they are important. The 14,000-foot, double-peaked Mount Shasta is very nearly the tallest peak in the range, and one of the showiest. For sheer spectacle, it rivals Alaska's Mount McKinley, a much bigger mountain. With five living glaciers clinging to its sides, Shasta's snowy top dominates the skyline north of Redding. Beyond its beauty, Shasta is important as the keystone of a vast watershed, whose water is impounded fifty miles to the south at Shasta Lake.

Smaller than Shasta, and perhaps not so striking, Mount Lassen brings its own kind of fame to the Cascades. It is the only volcano in the coterminous forty-eight states to erupt in the 20th century. Its 1915 eruption was enough to win it the 100-thousand-acre Lassen Volcanic National Park in which to show off its lava fields and steaming fissures.

South and east of Lassen begins the Sierra Nevada, a very different kind of mountain. In simplest geological terms, the Sierras are block mountains (in a sense *one* mountain) formed millions of years ago when the earth bulged to a height of 14 thousand feet and the bulge split at the top. The eastern portion slipped thousands of feet, exposing a wall of rock 300 miles long, now known as the eastern escarpment. On the western side, the slope of the Sierras is so gentle that in places it is scarcely perceptible.

The Spanish, who named "the great snowy ridge" probably never explored it. It was 1844 before Fremont led the first wagon train of Americans over the range, and it remained something of a barrier to immigration until the coming of the railroad in the 1860s. Even today there are only five roads through the Sierras, and most are closed by snow in winter.

Mark Twain, who as a young man explored the Sierras, observed, "There are just two seasons in the region — the breaking up of one winter and the beginning of the next." But the vast amount of snow is now looked upon with joy, not only for its beauty and the precious water it stores but also for its contribution to winter recreation areas like Squaw Valley and Echo Summit near Lake Tahoe.

The natural beauty of the Sierras and its preservation is inevitably linked with the name of John Muir, the great naturalist and founder of the Sierra Club. Muir was brought to California from Scotland as a child and spent most of his long life exploring and living in the Sierras, which he called "the range of light." It was largely through his efforts that vast areas in the range have come under federal protection as national parks, national forests, and wilderness areas. Muir's creed was simple. "Everyone," he said, "needs beauty as well as bread."

(Following Page:) A colorful cedar grove with wild gooseberry growing in a canyon in the California mountains.

One of Muir's early homes, and apparently his favorite, was Yosemite Valley, where he settled in 1860. Using this as a base, he explored places like King's Canyon and the Sequoia forests and published their existence to the world. Partly because of Muir's zeal of a century ago, the Sierras have become one of the most heavily used recreation areas in the country. It is estimated that in summer alone between 8 and 10 million persons visit and enjoy the parks and other public lands.

Muir spent a lifetime in the Sierras and never ran out of new things to see. In anyone's language the range is a wonderland of natural beauty, jagged granite peaks, and glacier-sculptured rock; forests of sequoia, lodgepole pine, red fir; thousands of deep blue lakes from big Tahoe down to nameless ponds; falls and torrents; deep-walled canyons; whole meadows of shooting star, lupine, larkspur; ouzels and hawks; ground squirrels and bighorn sheep; and, finally, the benign mountain light that moved Muir so deeply.

If the Sierras harbored nothing more than the great sequoias (Sequoiadendron giganteum), cousins of the coast redwoods, they would be worth crossing a continent to visit. The big trees are the earth's largest living things, some measuring forty feet in diameter and up to 300 feet in height.

Many Americans think of the destruction of natural beauty as a 20th century phenomenon. In the Sierras most of the damage was done in the last century, by hydraulic mining for gold in the foothills, grazing of sheep and cattle, clear cutting of forests. The Wilderness Act of 1964 should insure that these activities have ended forever on many public lands.

Today's young nature lover will be shocked to learn that the rock walls around Yosemite Falls were once painted with commercial advertising. His next trip to the falls may convince him that despite the crush of visitors, the lot of the nature lover has probably improved in the past century.

Across the Owens Valley from the Sierra Escarpment, in the Inyo National Forest, are the White Mountains which also reach a height of 14 thousand feet. Here grow the mysterious bristlecone pine, the oldest living things on earth. Some of the bristlecones in the Inyo Forest are thought to be four thousand years old. The mountains themselves, at a mere 180 million years, are considered young. Nature has no limit of paradoxes.

(Preceding Page:) In the town of Mendocino on the Northern California coast, an old water tower serves as a reminder of the area's New England heritage.

NORTHERN CALIFORNIA

OREGON

Crescent City

Clear Lake Res.

Yreka

Tule L

Goose L

LAVA BEDS NATIONAL MONUMENT

Canby

Upper L

Middle Alkali L

Weed

Mt. Shasta

Alturas

Dunsmuir

Lower L

Shasta L

Pit River

COAST

Klamath River

Trinity Mts.

Trinity River

Arcata

Eureka

Weaverville

Burney

Fortuna

Redding

Eagle L

RANGE

HUMBOLDT REDWOODS

Anderson

Lassen Pk.

Susanville

Lake Almanor

Red Bluff

LASSEN VOLCANIC NATIONAL PARK

Honey L

SACRAMENTO

Corning

Quincy

SIERRA

Fort Bragg

Eel River

Chico

Paradise

Mid. Fk. Yuba

Mendocino

Willows

Oroville

Feather River

Truckee

NEVADA

Ukiah

Clear L

Colusa

Marysville

Grass Valley

VALLEY

Lakeport

Sacramento River

Yuba City

Lake Tahoe

Cloverdale

Russian River

Roseville

Auburn

American River

Ft. Ross

Lake Beryessa

Woodland

Placerville

Healdsburg

Santa Rosa

SACRAMENTO

Bodega Bay

Stanislaus River

Tomales Bay

Napa

Pt. Reyes Nat. Seashore

Petaluma

Vallejo

Bodie

MUIR WOODS NAT. MON.

San Rafael

Lodi

Drakes Bay

Richmond

Stockton

Berkley

Mono L

San Francisco

Oakland

Merced River

YOSEMITE NATIONAL PARK

San Francisco Bay

Hayward

Modesto

White Mts.

San Mateo

Tuolumne

Lake Crowley

Half Moon Bay

Palo Alto

Turlock

DEVILS POSTPILE NAT. MON.

Santa Clara

Atwater

Bishop

San Jose

Merced

PACIFIC

Santa Cruz Mts.

Chowchilla

Santa Cruz

Los Banos

Madera

KINGS CANYON NATIONAL PARK

OCEAN

Monterey Bay

SAN

San Benito River

Pacific Grove

Salinas

JOAQUIN

Fresno

Monterey

Pt. Lobos

Carmel

Soledad

VALLEY

Big Sur

PINNACLES NAT. MON.

SOUTHERN CALIFORNIA

THE COAST

VIEWED from seaward, the coast of Northern California appears remarkably un-domesticated. Except at San Francisco, it is not a coast of snug harbors, broad estuaries, or navigable rivers, those deep and quiet backwaters which invite heavy human settlement and commerce. A great wall of rock rises from the ocean; hills and peaks glimpsed through breaks in the fog confirm that the wall is backed by a mightly continent. At scattered offshore rookeries, seals and sea lions define their turf with croaks and barks. Sea birds fly their tireless patrols in search of fish. Nature seems everywhere in command.

From driftwood-strewn Pelican Beach south to the jutting headlands of Big Sur, roughly 500 miles, there are only three significant breaks in the coastline, Humboldt Bay, Golden Gate, and Monterey Bay. It is not a coast that navigators are drawn to hug. Thousands of sharp rocks and a large, angry surf have claimed more than their share of imprudent or just plain unlucky mariners.

To describe a surf as *angry* is to seize upon a shop-worn metatphor. But, in this case, nothing else seems quite accurate. Robert Frost, a native Northern Californian, lived most of his adult life within a short distance of the Atlantic Ocean, and never seemed moved to draw upon it for imagery. But he retained from his childhood an image of the Northern California surf which symbolized for him nothing less than divine anger:

> The shattered water made a misty din.
> Great waves looked over others coming in,
> And thought of doing something to the shore
> That water never did to land before. *

---

*From "Once by the Pacific" by Robert Frost, *West-Running Brook*, New York, Henry Holt, 1928.

(Preceding Two Pages:) Spectacular color in the Sacramento Valley, the sun sets behind the California Coast Range at the confluence of the Feather River and the Sacramento River.

Seen from the landside, coastal Northern California could scarcely offer a more pleasant contrast. High above ragged headlands on gently rolling brown hills, beef cattle graze on chapparal and woodland grass and seek shade in stands of live oak. California poppies, violets, and lupine color hillside meadows. On neat seaside farms furrows run to the cliff's edge. Regions of lush dairy farms and pampered vineyards produce bucolic landscapes to rival Europe's. And in higher elevations of the Coast Range, herds of Roosevelt elk disregard both man and his works.

Most of California's coastline is privately owned and not accessible to the public. But state and federal governments have been able to salvage a few enclaves for public use. South of Crescent City for about thirty miles stretches the shore of Redwood National Park, the last sizeable stand of the tall Coast Redwoods (Sequoia sempervirens), which once dominated this coast from Southern Oregon to Big Sur. Nowhere is the voice of man so small and muffled as beneath these 300-foot giants. Visitors have long commented on the silence in the groves and perhaps acoustics engineers know the cause. But just to stand under a living tree which may have been a thousand years old in the time of Christ seems reason enough for silence.

South of Cape Mendocino, the westernmost point of the forty-eight contiguous states, is the experimental King Range National Conservation Area. In this part of the state, Highway 101 has carried the stream of commerce twenty miles inland through the Humboldt Redwoods. From Ferndale to Rockport is the most sparsely populated section of the north coast. In the King Range, the Bureau of Land Management is trying to determine whether a near wilderness area can sustain itself when limited recreational and commercial use is permitted.

From an elevation of four thousand feet, the land drops steeply through thick second-growth woodlands and grassy meadows. The absence of roads helps to isolate beaches. There is some belief that in the forested canyons, cadres of mountain lions and black bears are busily regaining their lost numbers. It looks as though wilderness is taking hold again, but only time will tell.

About thirty miles north of San Francisco, Point Reyes juts out sharply from suburban Marin County. It is the most distinct point of land on the entire coast and the federal government has designated the entire peninsula a national seashore. The eastern edge of the 64,000-acre preserve is defined by the San Andreas Fault. Beyond this point, the fault disappears beneath the ocean. Broad beaches, busy tidal pools, lonely dunes, and grass-covered headlands create a seascape that might look familiar to Sir Francis Drake. Drake is believed to have careened his ship *The Golden Hind* in Drake Bay, a few miles northwest of San Francisco Bay.

In addition to the extensive seashore, Point Reyes encompasses a large forest, where the Douglas fir of the north country and the Bishop pine of the south meet and flourish. The forest has helped turn the area into an important wildlife sanctuary. More than 300 species of birds and dozens of mammals have been identified within the park. Looking at Point Reyes today, it is hard to believe that less than twenty-five years ago housing developers were poised with their bulldozers ready to level the place.

(Above, Right:) An oak grove in San Benito County gives a golden luster to the California Coastal Range.

(Below:) In the Gabilan Range near Salinas, the stillness of Meadow Lake adds to the peacefulness of the valley.

(Right:) Trees take on the glitter of gold during the autumn months in Lake County, California.

With a decline in logging and fishing over the decades, the coast north of the Golden Gate has lost some of its former commercial importance, although tourism and recreation bid fair to take up that slack. Eureka, on Humboldt Bay, a town of only 25,000, is still the chief port between San Francisco and the Columbia River. In the late 19th century, when logging dominated the economy of the north coast, Eureka was a boom town. It is still a busy port for its size, but an atmosphere of past glory is evident. In fact, the town is developing the patina of an historic landmark. The Victorian mansions built by lumber barons are now the subject of a guided tour.

The tiny former doghole port of Mendocino, close to the oldest town on the north coast, also grew rich exporting lumber in the 19th century and then almost faded from existence. In recent years it has enjoyed a renaissance as an art colony and popular location for shooting Hollywood movies.

South of San Francisco the coast is more heavily populated. In suburbs like Pacifica, promontories are virtually covered with development housing. At Half Moon Bay the crowding diminishes and agriculture again dominates the landscape.

Broad curving Monterey Bay with its many beaches is one of the most popular vacation areas in California. At the south corner of the bay, the Monterey Peninsula has been attracting tourists — usually affluent ones — since the last century. Robert Louis Stevenson was one of the first to sing the praises of the Peninsula in the 1880s, and visitors have been coming to see for themselves ever since. But not even this heavy stream of human traffic can obscure the beauty and charm of the place.

Monterey was California's first capital and so can claim legitimate historic importance. Until the decline in sardine runs, it was an important fishing port. The vestiges of Cannery Row, immortalized in the fiction of John Steinbeck, still draw attention from tourists.

Carmel, at the other side of the Peninsula, has cultivated a kind of chic to supplement nature as a tourist draw. The presence of "colonies" of artists and writers has strengthened the image. Carmel's most durable attraction is the Carmel Mission, a well-preserved example of the many 18th-century Spanish missions which stretched almost the length of Caifornia. The famous missionary and explorer, Father Junipero Serra, who founded many of them, is buried here.

There is a state preserve at Point Lobos and here nature comes into her own again. Below Point Lobos begins the famous Big Sur coast. When the poet, Robinson Jeffers, first came to this area with his bride in 1914, they had to travel the last forty miles by horse-drawn mail stage, since no motor vehicle of that day could have negotiated the post road. In the half century since then, man has brought many changes to the coast, may even have done some damage, but has not diminished its fundamental majesty.

The overpowering surf continues its slow task of wearing away the headlands. The redwoods stand tall and straight; the graceful cypress yields and grows as the wind directs. Pelicans and cormorants fish from offshore rocks, and the bull sea lion keeps an eye on his hard-won harem. In spring the wildflowers — violets, roses, creamcups, poppies — envelop whole acres of Point Lobos.

Looking at all this Jeffers drew comfort from the smallness and impotence of man.

> . . . we know
> that the enormous invulnerable beauty of things
> Is the face of God, to live gladly in its presence, and die without
> grief or fear knowing it survives us.*

---

*From "Nova" by Robinson Jeffers, *The Selected Poetry of Robinson Jeffers,* New York, Random House, 1937.

(Above Right:) Napa Valley, famous for its rich vineyards and beautiful wineries, shows off its full color range in autumn.

(Below:) Navarro River flows in from the Pacific Ocean as seen from Navarro Ridge.

(Right:) Above broad wooded valleys, viewed from the Sacramento River, Mt. Shasta stands out at 14,162 feet.

(Left:) Massive granite domes and spires of Castle Crags State Park rise above an evergreen forest near Mt. Shasta.

(Above:) From the north, snow-covered Mt. Shasta is a breath-taking sight from the valleys below.

(Below:) Near Redding, Shasta Dam was built to create a lake from the Sacramento River. The man-made lake is now one of California's most popular boating resorts.

(Above, Right:) A cable car coming up Hyde Street in San Francisco from the pier where ferry boats take you to Angel Island. Alcatraz is seen in the background.

(Below:) An evening view of San Francisco from the Bay Bridge on Yerba Buena Island.

(Right:) Colorful fall cottonwoods in Owens Valley near Bishop looking west. The Sierras can be seen in the background.

(Above:) Rusty pipes and wreckage below Steinbeck's famous Cannery Row in Monterey.
(Below:) Monterey cypress seem to grow from the rocks on a sea bluff in Carmel.
(Right:) Heavy cumulus clouds and fog add to the beauty along the Big Sur coast in Central California.
(Following Two Pages:) Fog and wind blow briskly over the 99 mile stretch of rugged Big Sur coastline.

(Left:) Surf comes in below the Bixby Creek bridge along the Big Sur coast, while threatening clouds darken the skies above.
(Above:) Yucca whipplei, *commonly known as Our Lord's Candle, is an elegant sight on the hillside of Big Sur.*
(Below:) Sun shining through the fog over Big Sur from Post Road.

(Above, Left:) A Heerman's Gull perches on the moss covered rocks at Moss Landing.
(Above, Right:) Boats rise and fall in the tide at Moss Landing Harbor on Monterey Bay.
(Below, Left:) Coit Tower as seen from San Francisco's Fisherman's Wharf.
(Below, Right:) A peaceful lagoon on Wadell Creek, south of San Francisco on the San Mateo County coast.
(Right:) Among the trees in General Grant Grove, Kings Canyon Nat. Park, General Grant tree seems to stand out alone.

(Left:) Roaring River Falls in King's Canyon National Park.

(Right:) From an underground creek, Burney Falls drops into a churning pool below.

(Below:) Snow covers a dominant peak in the California mountains as fog rises on its flank.

(Left:) A twisted bristlecone pine tree is a dramatic portrait against the brilliant blue sky in California's White Mountains.

(Right:) A quiet sunset on the Kings River at Zumwalt Meadow in King's Canyon National Park.

(Below:) California Bristlecone Pine Forest located in the White Mountains.

(Following Two Pages:) Half Dome is the most familiar monolith in Yosemite Valley — having a sheer face caused by glacier action.

(*Above:*) *Lone Jeffrey pine at the top of Sentinel Dome, Yosemite.*
(*Below:*) *Cathedral Peak reigns over Tuolumne Meadows, the largest sub-Alpine meadow in the High Sierra, elevation 8600 feet.*
(*Right:*) *The Three Brothers catch the morning light in Yosemite Valley. The same fascination remains as in 1851 when the valley was first entered by militia.*

(Left:) Mt. Dana towers 13,050 feet above sea level as seen from snow fed Tioga Lake in Yosemite National Park.

(Below:) Spring turns Yosemite Falls into a roaring torrent of snowmelt which falls 1,430 feet to the lush valley floor.

(Right:) El Capitan and its western buttress form part of the valley's Northern Rim with snow hummocks along the Merced River in the foreground.

(Following Two Pages:) Lake Tahoe's cold azure waters at Sand Point are rimmed by majestic sugar pines.

(Left:) Emerald Bay, on the west shore of Lake Tahoe, reflects sunlight from its deep waters.
(Above:) Mono Lake, east of the Sierra Nevada, has no outlet and brackish waters and salt columns bear witness to higher water levels of this dying lake.
(Below:) Ancient lava flows formed Devils Postpile, an 800-foot-long colonnade of hexagonal basaltic columns rising out of the California forests.

(Preceding Page, Left:) East of the Sierra, Bishop Creek runs down the winter slope to join the Owens River.
(Preceding Page, Right:) Like Bishop, Rock Creek runs into the Owens River and is picked up by an aqueduct to Los Angeles.
(Above:) A view up Middle fork of Bishop Creek.
(Below:) Snow covered Mt. Lassen at 10,457' shows a mirror image on Reflection Lake.
(Right:) Rockslides that have rolled down the mountain in the Bumpas Hell area of Lassen Volcanic National Park.

(Above:) An old barn stirs memories of ranching in the rolling hills of Sonoma Valley, north of San Francisco.
(Below:) The plowed fields in San Lorenzo Valley — south Monterey County show the richness of California's fertile soil.
(Right:) The Coast Redwoods in Redwood National Park on Highway 101 are older and taller than any other trees in California.

THE LAKES

NORTHERN CALIFORNIA is not usually associated in the popular mind with lakes as Minnesota or Wisconsin might be. Yet, it can claim some of the most beautiful mountain lakes in the country. Some of the largest and most striking have been man made through the damming of rivers; a few natural lakes have been enlarged by the same means. But even these man-made bodies of water seem to blend well with their setting and improve the beauty of the landscape.

Traditionally, lakes in California are treated with care by government and citizen alike. It is a state with chronic water problems, and many of its major lakes were created principally to impound the lifegiving water.

Lakes are among the most short-lived and delicate of natural land features. Limnologists tell us, in fact, that lakes are supposed to disappear in the course of time, silting up and giving way to forests. Geological evidence suggests that Yosemite Valley was once covered by a large lake. The Mojave Desert in Southern California is checkered with the beds of quite large lakes which dried up in the unknown past. If interfered with by man, even a large lake can sometimes disappear within the span of a human lifetime, as has Tulare Lake in Kings County.

Though there are lakes in all parts of Northern California, most, as might be expected, are to be found in the Cascade or Sierra Nevada Ranges. and this includes some of the largest artificial ones. Lake Tahoe, which extends into Nevada, is certainly the best known of California lakes and perhaps the most beautiful, if such things can be measured. If we may judge from the written comments of visitors from Mark Twain onward, this must be so.

Tahoe is a natural lake and the prototype of a mountain lake. At six thousand feet elevation, it sits in a ring of forested mountains. It is twenty-three miles long, thirteen miles wide, and more than 1500 feet deep in its deepest parts. It is extraordinarily blue in all seasons. Tahoe's great depth may account for its not freezing over in winter.

The explorer John Fremont first named it Bonpland in the 1840s to honor a French botanist. In 1852, it was renamed Lake Bigler to honor California's governor. But during the Civil War the governor proved to be a Copperhead, and an angry mapmaker on his own initiative again renamed the lake. He chose the Washoe Indian word for "big water," and so it became Tahoe, a major improvement in both significance and euphony.

The discovery of the Comstock Lode in nearby Nevada resulted in a stampede of gold prospectors through the area in the mid 19th century and they seriously threatened the ecology. The mountains on the Nevada side were stripped of their forests to supply timbers for the mines at Virginia City. Once the mining had declined, however, the forests began to grow back.

Today, Tahoe faces another threat, urbanization. Carson City, Nevada, has stretched out westward to envelop the eastern shore with condominiums and night clubs. Since Tahoe is one of the most popular recreation centers in the West, summer and winter, there is much concern about pollution of the natural environment. On the California side a National Forest offers some measure of protection and the great depth of the lake, too, may help it survive the impact of modern American life.

Clear Lake, the largest natural lake lying entirely within California, is not in the western mountains as might be expected but in the Coast Range north of Santa Rosa. It is about 100 square miles in area and may have been two lakes in prehistoric times. The presence of hot springs in the area suggests that volcanic activity may have played a role in the lake's formation.

For more than a century, agricultural activity has been heavy at Clear Lake, both grazing and farming. By the 1940s, the accumulation of insecticides and fertilizers in the lake has dangerously affected its ecological balance. Prompt action by the state, especially the introduction of fresh-water smelt, has reversed the decline and the lake is rapidly regaining its former vigor. It is a major recreation area.

Lake Shasta, north of Redding, is the largest man-made lake in California. It was created by the damming of the powerful Upper Sacramento River and covers an area of 30,000 acres. The lake is also fed by the Pit and McCloud Rivers. Lake Shasta is the pivot of the Central Valley project for flood control, irrigation and water conservation. It has also developed into one of the largest and most popular recreation areas in the state. Lake Shasta is so large that even in heavily populated California, it does not appear crowded with vacationers. Among sportsmen, Shasta is perhaps best known for its great variety of game fish, some sixteen in all.

Among the other major man-made lakes are Oroville, Clair Engle, Lewiston, Berryessa, Folsom, Almanor, McClure, and Isabella. The waters of Lake Oroville are held by the country's highest dam and one of the world's highest at 770 feet. The lake is fed by the three branches of the Feather River, the greatest water flow out of the Sierra Nevada.

Lake Berryessa in Napa County is close to the Bay area and is much used by city

(Left:) An unusual pattern formed by ironstone ridges can be seen at Drakes Beach, Pt. Reyes National Seashore.

(Right:) The Pacific Ocean washes through a sea arch on the Mendocino headlands cutting it away until it becomes a completely severed sea stack.

(Below:) A line of breakers at North Beach, Pt. Reyes National Seashore.

people. Its relatively warm waters support year-round fishing. Folsom Lake, made by damming the American River, is relatively new. It is close to Sacramento and is much used by people from the capital city for recreation. Almanor was once California's largest man-made lake.

Mono Lake, at the foot of the Sierra Escarpment and bordered by Highway 395, is probably not an American's idea of a lake. Its mineral heavy waters support no fish, and it has been called a "second Dead Sea." The title is not inappropriate; Mono's barren shore area, with its curious tufa towers, might indeed stir memories of the Dead Sea. Evaporation has reduced its extent and further concentrated its mineral content. Now deprived of the fresh water streams which used to feed it, Mono Lake, still close to 100 square miles in area, will continue to evaporate until it becomes a dry lake bed like those in the Mojave.

Another shallow lake but of a very different sort is Tule Lake in the extreme north end of the state. Tule is very shallow and is what would be called in Central Europe a steppe lake. It used to be much larger than its present 12,000 acres, but ill-conceived Federal land reclamation projects early in the century caused a sizeable portion of it to be drained and put to the plow. Fortunately the drainage schemes were halted and the area turned into a National Wildlife Refuge. Each year, Tule witnesses the largest gathering of waterfowl in the world. Two neighboring lakes, Clear and Lower Klamath are also National Wildlife Refuges.

For all its present beauty and serenity, Tule Lake has known some unpleasant history. In the 19th century, it was the setting for the bloody Modoc Wars, when the Modoc Indians resisted being driven from their homeland. Again in 1942, Tule came to national attention. Thousands of Japanese-Americans were herded into a concentration camp at nearby Newell.

Within the Lassen Volcanic National Park are many small and medium sized lakes formed when glacier-gouged depressions filled with runoff. They are known collectively as the Lassen Lakes though a few like Manzanita, Juniper and Snag are distinct enough to have established their own reputations. Some of the Lassen Lakes are fed by hot springs or heated by subterranean volcanic activity. Others are glacier cold. Few of the lakes have natural outlets and they do not support fish populations reliably. However, the lakes are sufficiently popular as providing a striking setting for the volcanic peak.

Eagle Lake, east of Mount Lassen, is the second largest natural lake within the state's borders and something of an ecological curiosity. Sitting at 5,000 feet above sea level, Eagle is nevertheless a vestige of a prehistoric inland sea that once covered this part of Lassen County. Its slightly alkaline waters will not support most fish, either game or coarse, though it has been stocked many times. Inexplicably, the only game fish that can survive in its waters is the resident Eagle Lake trout, which can be found nowhere else in the world. There is some evidence to suggest that the Eagle Lake trout may be a prehistoric species. One of the few other creatures to flourish in the lake is a sea snail which can clearly be traced to prehistoric times. Unique species of reptiles and small mammals have been found around the shores of the lake. Like Tule Lake, Eagle has been the victim of crackpot drainage schemes in years past and as a consequence has lost some of its size.

The most mysteriously misnamed lake is Honey, a large lake in southeast Lassen County. Its bitter waters support no life and the name may even have been some pioneer's idea of a joke. Honey Lake is broad but very shallow. In periods of drought it has been known to dry up completely.

Donner Lake, northwest of Tahoe, is chiefly interesting because of associations with the ill-fated Donner Party. It lies in a beautiful forested basin, scoured by the glacier, just east of the seven thousand foot Donner Pass. In 1846, the stranded Donner Party camped for months in the deep snows around its shore. Little more than half the group ever made it into the valley.

Big Lagoon and its fellows, Stone and Freshwater, border Highway 101 along the coast north of Arcata. Their principal charm is their proximity to the Pacific surf. No more than a sand spit separates Big Lagoon from the ocean, not unlike the ponds on Cape Cod in Massachusetts. The lagoons may have been formed when the surf pushed a high sand spit in the path of freshwater streams pouring out of the coastal forests. In the 1850s, this area became the object of a hysterical gold rush when it was announced in San Francisco that the sands of the beach were laced with gold. The sands do in fact contain gold but in such small quantities that it cannot be extracted economically. After the gold rush, the lagoons and adjacent beaches settled back to the tranquility that they enjoy to this day.

(Following Page:) Poppies grow wild in a field at San Gregorio Valley near the coast.

THE VALLEY

THE GREAT CENTRAL VALLEY, 450 miles long and an average of forty miles wide, lies mostly in Northern California. It is the world's richest agricultural area, and its diversity of crops — fruit, vegetables, grain, grapes, cotton, and more — is unmatched. The valley is protected by a continuous mountain wall, broken only by San Francisco Bay. Unlike the case of the mountains, scenic beauty in the valley is mostly man-made. It is a carefully tended, giant garden.

The northern section, drained by the Sacramento River, is properly the Sacramento Valley, and the southern end, the San Joaquin Valley. Sacramento, the state capital, owes its place of honor to its proximity to the first goldfields in mother lode country of the Sierra foothills to the east. In fact, the city was founded by Captain John Sutter in 1839, and, in effect, this is where the history of modern California began.

With an assist from the engineers, Sacramento, and Stockton on the San Joaquin River, have become deep-water ports. Since the end of World War II, both cities have moved to diversify their economies, which were totally allied to agriculture, and some light industry has sprung up. But it will always be agriculture that makes the wheels turn in the valley.

The most glamorous product of the valley, and probably the biggest money maker, is wine. The vineyards are concentrated in the San Joaquin, and the towns of Lodi, Modesto, Madera, and Fresno have become major centers of winemaking and distribution. The new mass production methods used by big wineries like A. & J. Gallo, United Vintners, and Guild would turn the hair of a vineyard master in France. But the methods have paid off in millions of gallons of good bulk table wines at low prices.

Most visitors agree that the meticulously ordered vineyards stretching for miles across the floor of the San Joaquin are one of the scenic treats of California. To further cheer the

(Preceding Page:) The most photographed victorian home in the state, the 18 room Carson Mansion in Eureka was built in the 1880s.

tourist, most wineries maintain tasting rooms, where guests are invited to sample the wines. Many of the wineries offer guided tours, as well.

Seen from the air, the central valley is a mammoth tapestry of green and brown geometric patterns, groves, vineyards, and fields, bordered by rivers, irrigation canals, highways, and fences. From Red Bluff to Visalia, the sun-baked towns are laid out on a north-south axis along Interstate 5 and old U.S. 50 like the vertebrae of a gigantic spine, the backbone of Northern California. The central valley cannot rival the infinite and subtle beauties of a Point Lobos or a Tuolumne Gorge. Still, it has its own kind of glamour.

(Left:) Russian Orthodox Church, Ft. Ross Chapel burned twice in 1825 and 1970. The new construction was completed in 1974.

(Below:) Bodie, a ghost town located north of Mono Lake, had its heyday in 1878 when a rich vein was discovered and a total of $21,000,000 was mined from the area.

(Above, Left:) Father Serra lies buried under the altar of perhaps the most beautiful of the California missions located in Carmel.
(Above, Right:) Poppies, California's state flower, grow wild along the Big Sur coast.
(Below, Left:) The headframe of the Kennedy Mine, at Jackson, can be seen in the distant view of this abandoned tailing wheel.
(Below, Right:) Fisherman's Wharf, Monterey is a collection of shops and restaurants that contrast greatly with the historic town and Cannery Row located nearby.

SAN FRANCISCO AND THE BAY AREA

S AN FRANCISCO and the dozen or so cities that ring San Francisco Bay are known collectively as the Bay Area. These include San Mateo, Palo Alto, Hayward, Alameda, Oakland, Richmond, Berkeley, and others. They share one of the largest landlocked harbors in the world — and one of the most beautiful. Actually, there are three bays: San Francisco, San Pablo, and Suisun, which add up to 450 square miles. Originally, the bay was larger than this, but it is constantly being reduced by landfill. Richly endowed by nature to satisfy the needs of trade, the Bay Area has become, inevitably, a major center of population.

Built on twenty-nine small hills at the end of a peninsula, San Francisco has dominated the area since the Spanish established its predecessor, Yerba Buena, on the site. The city that everyone loves, it has been called. That is sweeping praise, but it is truly hard to find a person who doesn't love the place.

San Francisco has been much complimented by some Americans for not seeming like an American city at all. But this gauche compliment has less to do with the city's rich ethnic mix than with its incomparable physical setting, the broad bay, the brown hills, blue Pacific to the west, and the Golden Gate itself. All in all, a tough act for Kansas City and Indianapolis to try to match.

This world city has kept size and distance manageable. The land area is less than forty-five square miles, as compared to Chicago's 228 or New York's 320. It can't be much more than a mile from Fisherman's Wharf to the Trans-America Pyramid, incomparably different worlds. Chinatown is a five-minute walk from Nob Hill. In spite of the presence of tall buildings and the two great bridges, the city conveys a feeling of being committed to the human scale. That's why the few remaining cable cars make sense, even though they may function mainly as tourist attractions.

Officially, San Francisco's climate is described as temperate, a subtle way of saying that it never gets warm. Fogs are frequent and notorious, especially in summer. Winds can spring up without warning and turn a sunny August day into a bone-chiller. Then they will die down as suddenly as they came. Residents insist that it's all very invigorating.

San Francisco is a center of intellectual and cultural life. Its people take pride in their sophistication and artistic taste, and they can be brutally patronizing toward those Southern Californians whom they view as non-cerebral, sun-and-surf-struck Angelenos. But along with the sophistication comes a kind of fatalism, and not without reason. Anyone old enough to read knows that the city sits atop the San Andreas Fault and that tension in the fault has already reached maximum levels. It is a matter of *when* rather than *if* it is to generate a major earthquake. The local attitude seems to be, "we may have only one day to live, but at least we will live it in San Francisco."

Many writers have celebrated the virtues and even confessed the vices of the city, among them Charles Caldwell Dobie, George Sterling, Jack London, Herbert Asbury, Gertrude Atherton, Lawrence Ferlinghetti, and Herb Caen. San Franciscans love their city with a quiet determination, and they are jealous of her beauty. The truncated Embarcadero Freeway is a monument to their will to preserve as much of it as they can.

Geographically, the Bay Area is more intimately linked with the central valley than with other places along the coast. Through the great delta, where the Sacramento and San Joaquin rivers meet, the entire drainage of the interior empties into the Bay. In turn, the wind tunnel of the Golden Gate helps to air-condition parts of the interior. The cooling ocean winds which reach into the Sonoma and Napa Valleys make possible the kind of climate needed for the production of premium table wines.

Recently the federal government established the Golden Gate National Recreation Area, a unique park facility which is still in development. It comprises miscellaneous former federal military reservations, beaches, islands in the bay, museums, and some state and county lands, in all about 35,000 acres. Included in the preserve is some undeveloped coastline in Marin County, across the Golden Gate and only minutes from downtown San Francisco. The Golden Gate Recreation Area is the first of its kind in the country and may prove to be a blueprint for the development of recreational lands close to big cities.

(Following Page:) Sunset over the Pacific at Trinidad on the Northern Coast.